THE POLDARK COLOURING BOOK

The Official BBC Poldark Companions

The World of Poldark by Emma Marriott
Poldark: The Complete Scripts – Series One by Debbie Horsfield
The Poldark Colouring Book

The Poldark novels by Winston Graham

Ross Poldark • *Demelza* • *Jeremy Poldark* •
Warleggan • *The Black Moon* • *The Four Swans* •
The Angry Tide • *The Stranger from the Sea* •
The Miller's Dance • *The Loving Cup* •
The Twisted Sword • *Bella Poldark*

Also by Winston Graham

Night Journey • *The Merciless Ladies* •
The Forgotten Story • *Take My Life* • *Cordelia* •
Night Without Stars • *Fortune Is a Woman* •
The Little Walls • *The Sleeping Partner* • *Greek Fire* •
The Tumbled House • *Marnie* • *The Grove of Eagles* •
After the Act • *The Walking Stick* • *Angell, Pearl and Little God* •
The Japanese Girl (short stories) • *Woman in the Mirror* •
The Green Flash • *Cameo* • *Stephanie* •
Tremor • *The Ugly Sister*

The Spanish Armada • *Poldark's Cornwall* •
Memoirs of a Private Man

THE POLDARK

COLOURING BOOK

ILLUSTRATED BY GWEN BURNS

B📗XTREE

First published 2016 by Boxtree
an imprint of Pan Macmillan
20 New Wharf Road, London N1 9RR
Associated companies throughout the world
www.panmacmillan.com

ISBN 978-0-7522-6625-1

Illustrations by Gwen Burns

Pan Macmillan does not have any control over, or any responsibility for,
any author or third-party websites referred to in or on this book.

1 3 5 7 9 8 6 4 2

A CIP catalogue record for this book is available from the British Library.

Printed in Italy

Visit **www.panmacmillan.com** to read more about all our books
and to buy them. You will also find features, author interviews and
news of any author events, and you can sign up for e-newsletters
so that you're always first to hear about our new releases.